PRESIDENT DONALD TRUMP
A Patriot's Coloring Book

M.G. Anthony

Foreword by Nick Adams

A POST HILL PRESS BOOK

**President Donald Trump:
A Patriot's Coloring Book**
© 2017 by M.G. Anthony
All Rights Reserved

ISBN: 978-1-68261-454-9

No part of this book may be reproduced, stored in a retrieval system, or transmitted by any means without the written permission of the author and publisher.

Post Hill Press
New York • Nashville
posthillpress.com

Published in the United States of America

FOREWORD

On January 20, 2017, Donald J. Trump was sworn in as the 45th President of the United States. I was there.

Among the record crowd, there were incredible levels of excitement, anticipation and relief. Most notable, though, was the supercharged patriotism.

Never before had I seen so many American flags. Never before had an Inaugural Address experienced chants of "USA... USA... USA...".

In fact, one of President Trump's first acts was to personally issue *Proclamation 9570*, which designates the day of his inauguration as *National Day of Patriotic Devotion*.

The proclamation begins: "*A new national pride stirs the American soul and inspires the American heart. We are one people, united by a common destiny and a shared purpose.*"

Just a month later, in his first State of the Union Address, President Trump once more put patriotism front and center of his new leadership:

> *My job is not to represent the world; my job is to represent the United States of America...*
>
> *The time for small thinking is over. The time for trivial fights is behind us. We just need the courage to share the dreams that fill our hearts ... and the confidence to turn those hopes and those dreams into action.*
>
> *From now on, America will be empowered by our aspirations, not burdened by our fears. Inspired by the future, not bound by failures of the past, and guided by a vision, not blinded by our doubts. I am asking all citizens to embrace this renewal of the American spirit. I am asking all members of Congress to join me in dreaming big and bold... I'm asking everyone watching ... to seize this moment, believe in yourselves, believe in your future, and believe once more in America.*"

For those of us who love America, we are overjoyed by this renewed embrace of national pride.

I have always believed that among America's most magnificent assets was its patriotism; something that set it apart from every other country on this earth, even its English-speaking cousins.

As an American immigrant, it is not uncommon for me to look at the American flag and have my eyes well with tears. I love this country for so many reasons.

A rejection of patriotism, and an ambivalence of feeling toward the United States by Americans troubles me deeply.

It's why I set up FLAG—The Foundation for Liberty and American Greatness—a 501(c)(3), a non-partisan, non-profit, educational organization, that visits elementary, middle and high schools teaching students American values and spreading American patriotism.

FLAG is thrilled to present to you this historic coloring book.

May God bless you, your family and the exceptional nation of this earth – the United States of America.

Nick Adams
Founder and Executive Director,
FLAG
July 2017

Winning the Lottery of Life

I'm an immigrant to the United States.
I came here because this is the greatest country in the world.
I came here to make, and not take.
To give, and not receive.
To join the American way of life, not change it.
I came here because this is the one place where personality has not yet been downsized.
Where I can be myself.
Where people are still free to color outside the lines.
Where you can be a Christian, and refer to God without being looked at strangely.
Where people chase greatness and disdain mediocrity.
Where getting ahead requires kicking butt, not kissing it.
Where success and boldness is cherished, not resented.
Where optimism is the norm, and pessimists are rare.

I came here for freedom. For tradition. For opportunities and possibilities present nowhere else.

I'm here because in America, I am most free to chase my dreams.

I'm here, because in America, you can fall down 5000 times, and still get up 5001, if you have grit, determination and hustle.

I'm here because this is where the magic happens. Where you or your ideas or your mission can catch fire, and people support you and help you and promote you.

Why do millions of people from all over the world come to the United States, more than to anywhere else? Because no other nation has a culture so accommodating of potential and success.

Nowhere else can so many come with nothing and achieve anything.

Anyone can rise above the circumstances to achieve anything they want. This is the best place for anyone to live—black, white, Hispanic, gay, transgender, Muslim—or a combination.

And yes, I'm here because I love guns, hotdogs, chicken fried steak, barbecue, cheerleaders, American football, small town parades, beauty pageants, pick-up trucks, muscle cars and 16-lane freeways lined with the supersized American flags.

If you can make it here, you can make it anywhere. I came here because I wanted to be the best. And to be the best, you've got to learn from the best and mix it with the best, in order to be the best.

America improves you. America motivates you. America increases you.

It's the greatest country in the world.

The day anyone is born in, or moves permanently to the United States, is the day they win the lottery of life.

The day I won the lottery was the 29th of July, 2016.

When was yours?

Nick Adams

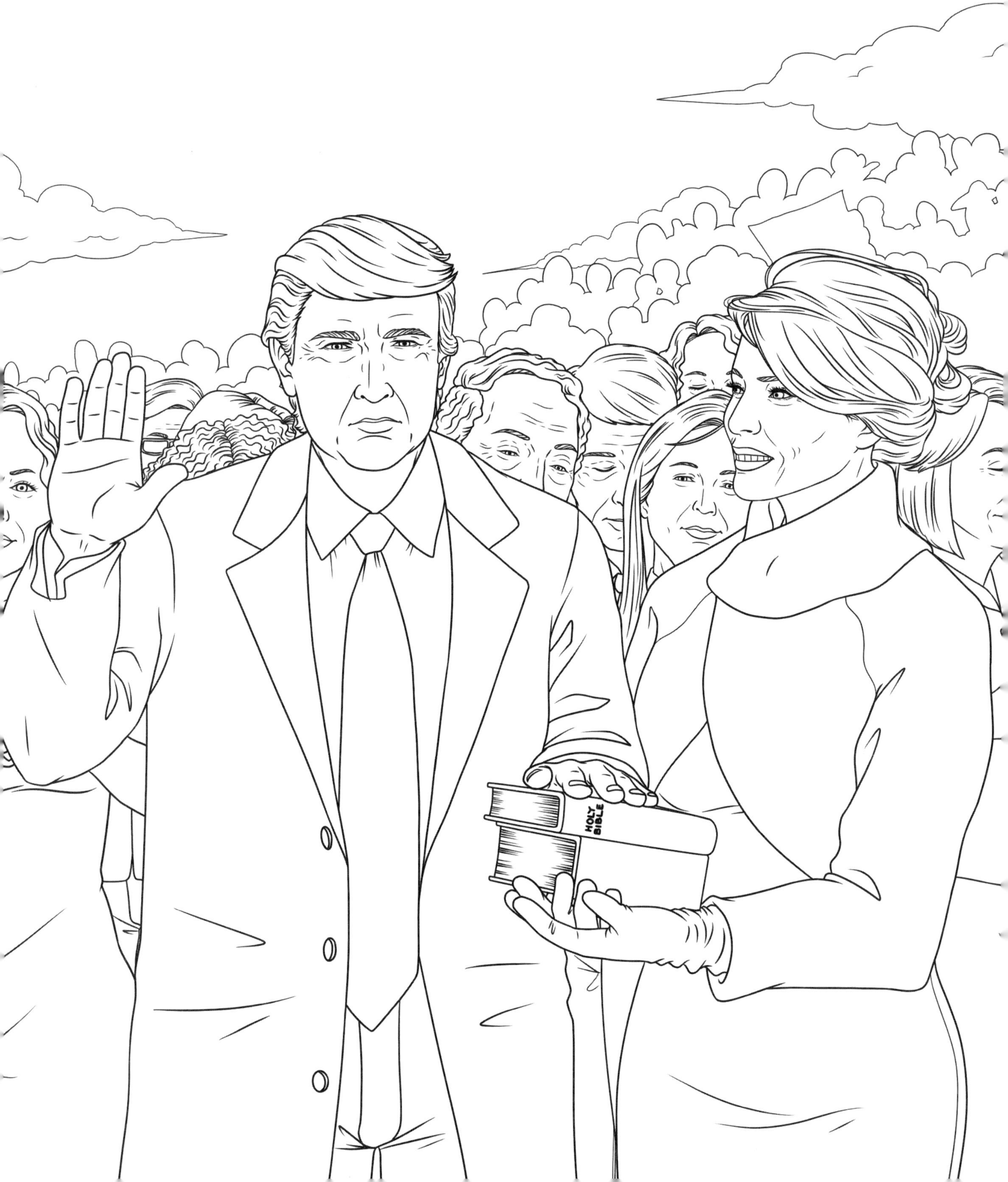
HOLY BIBLE

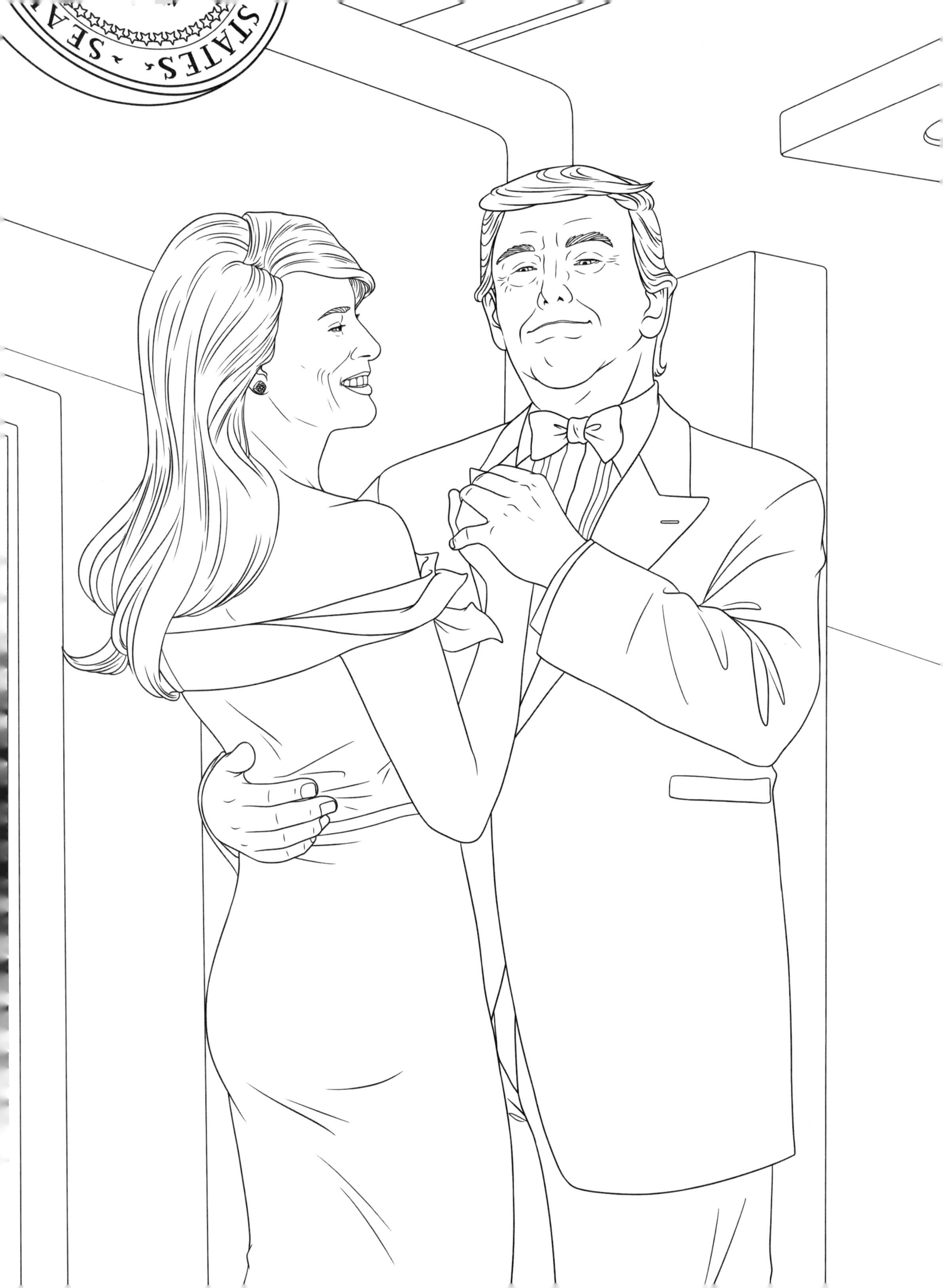
STATES

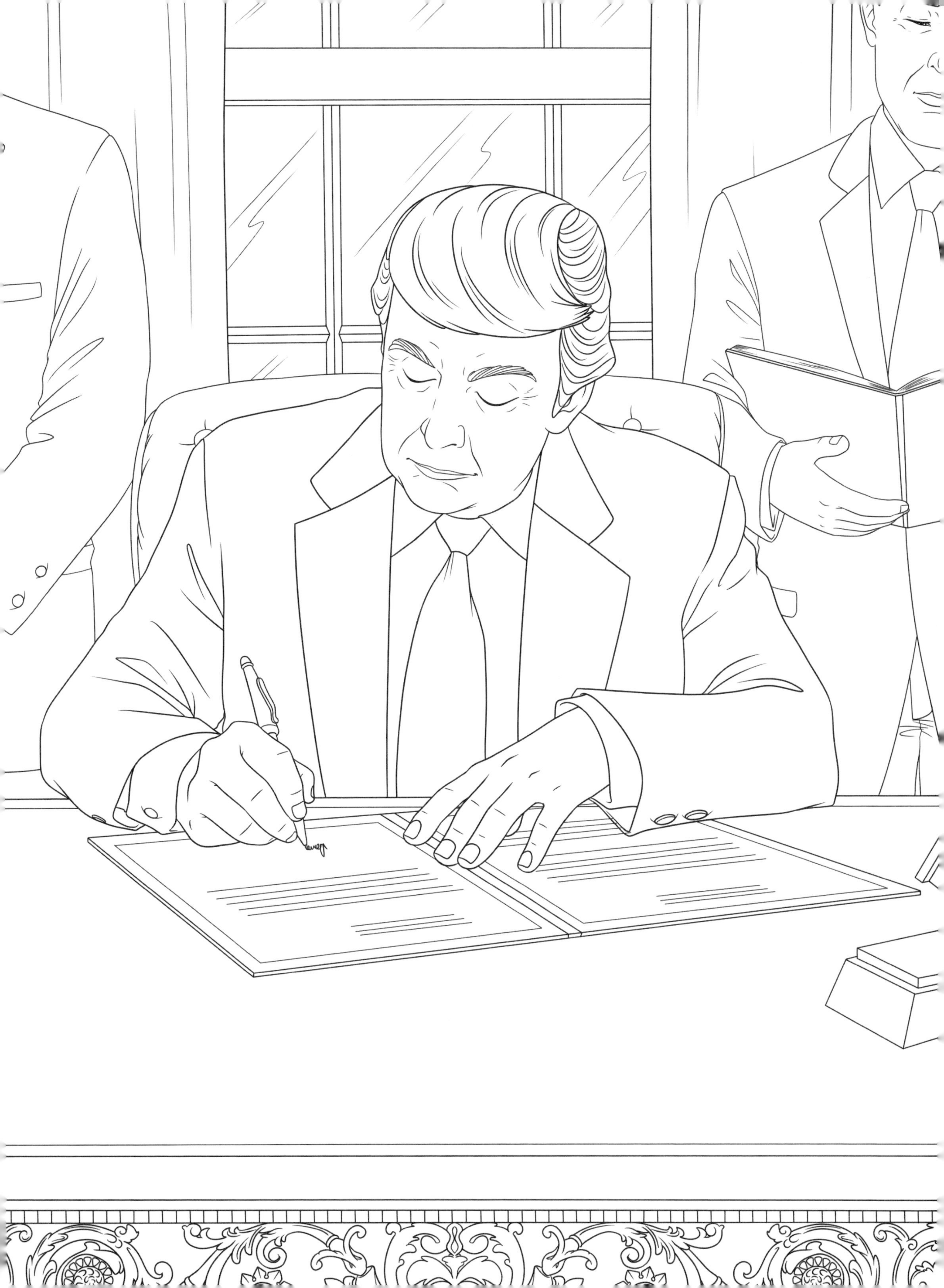

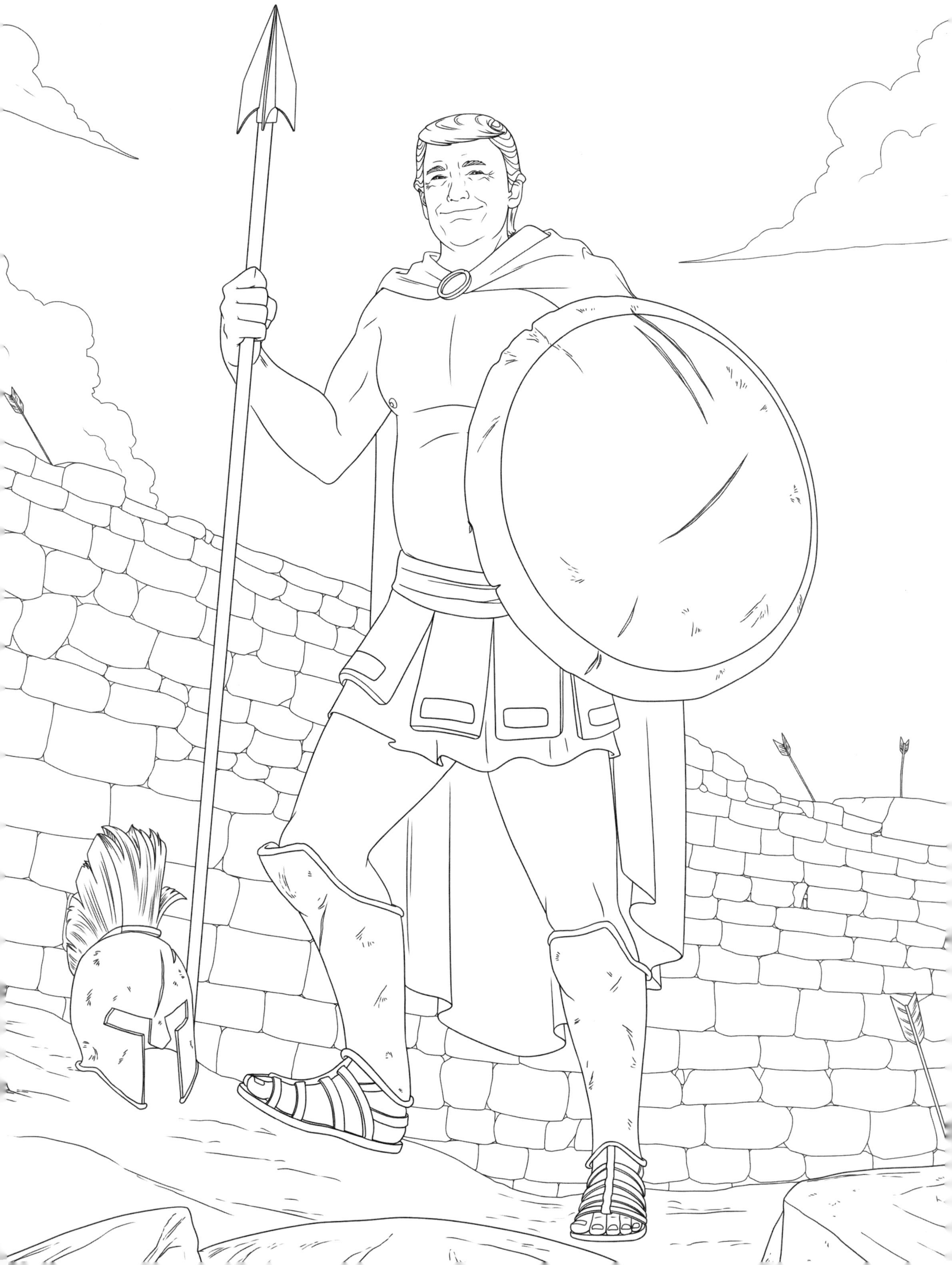

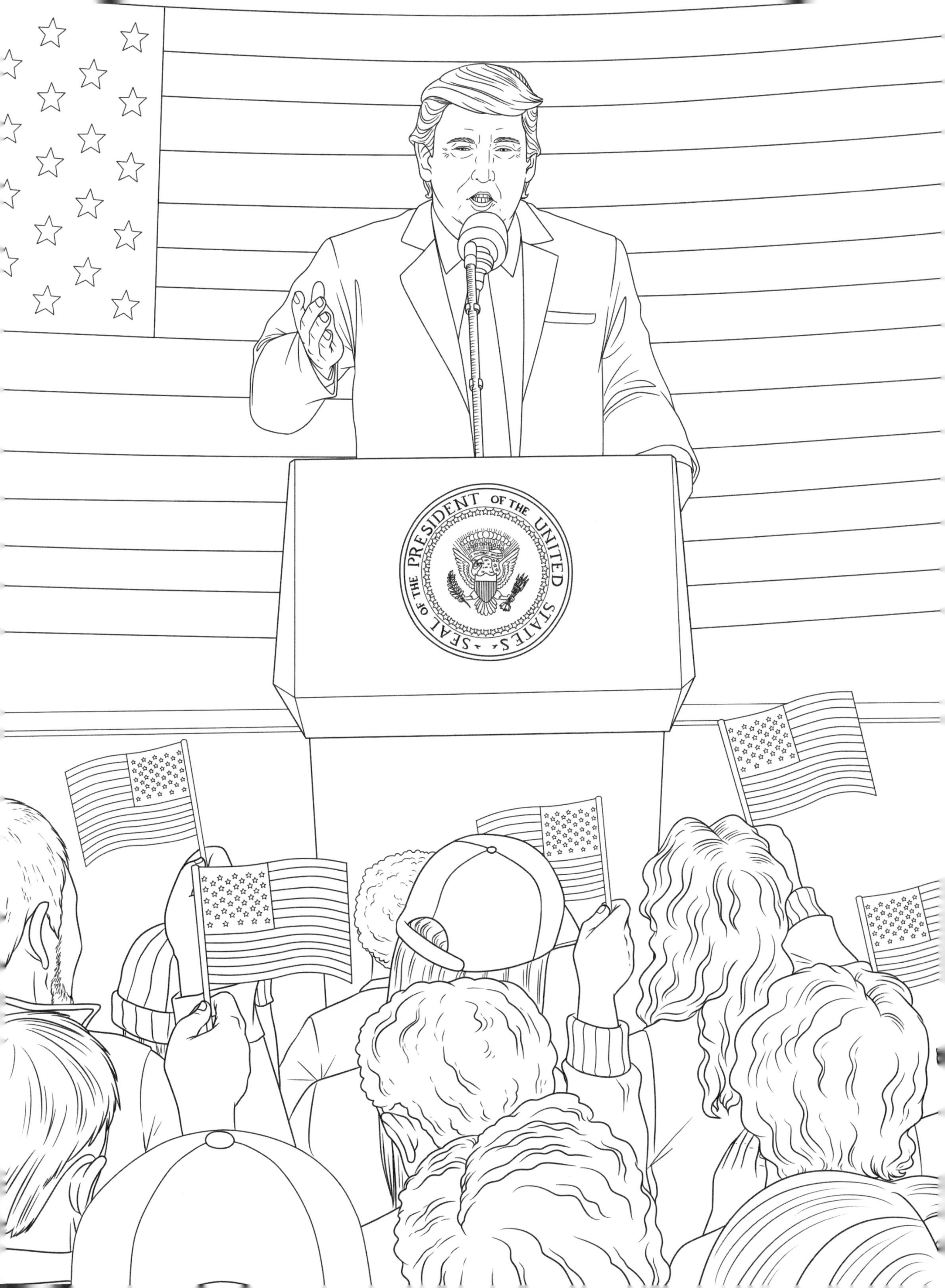
SEAL OF THE PRESIDENT OF THE UNITED STATES

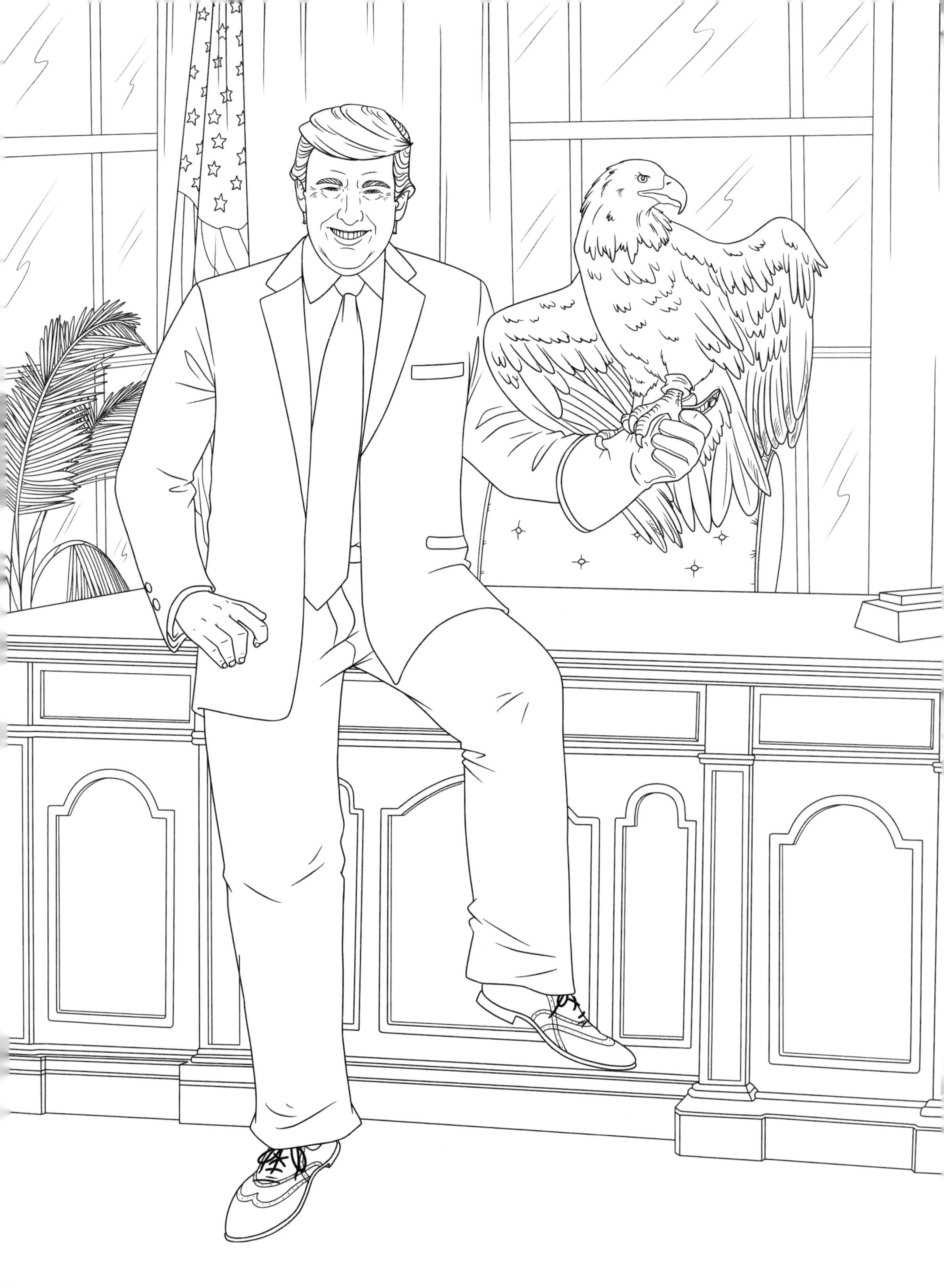

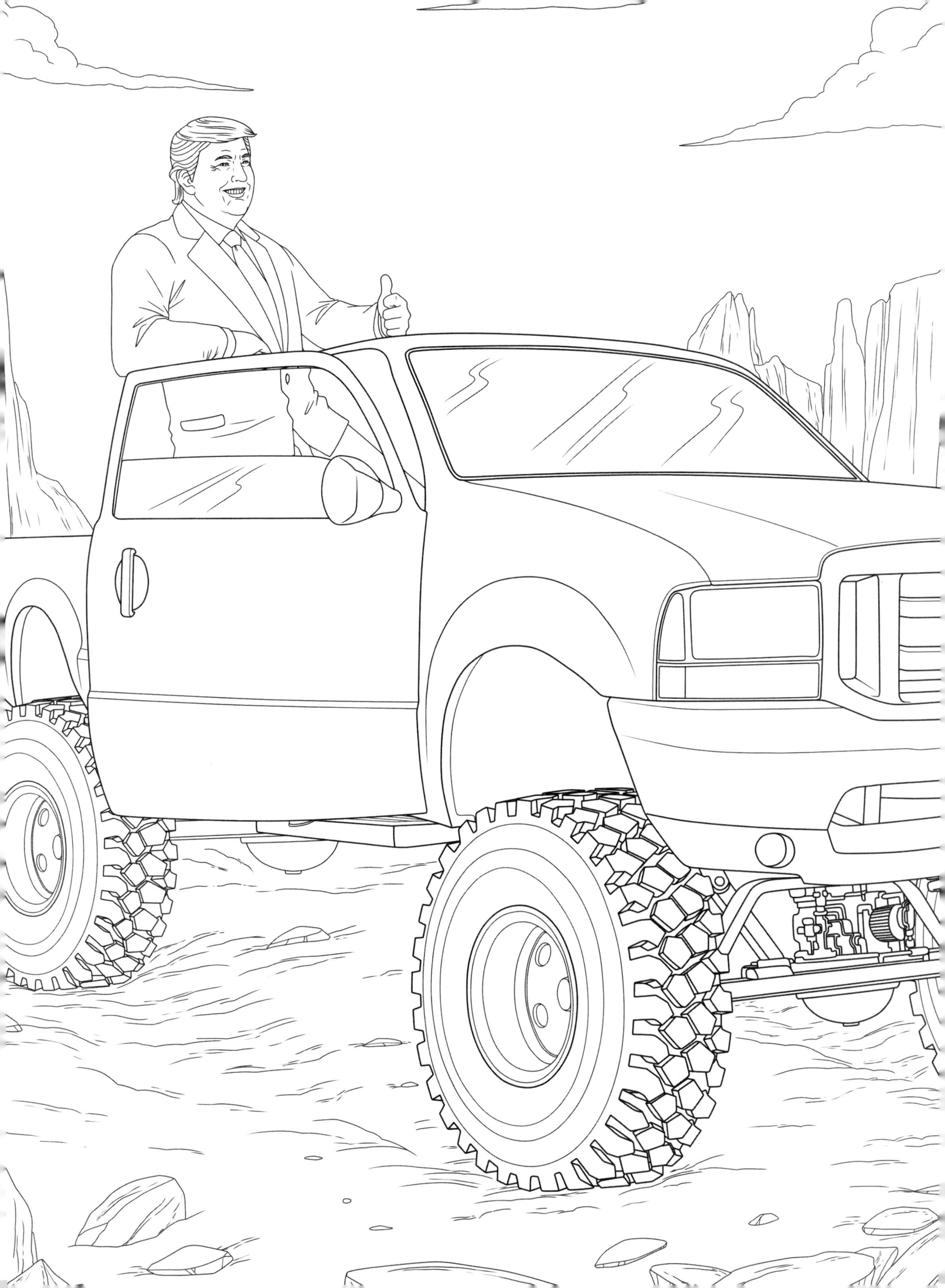

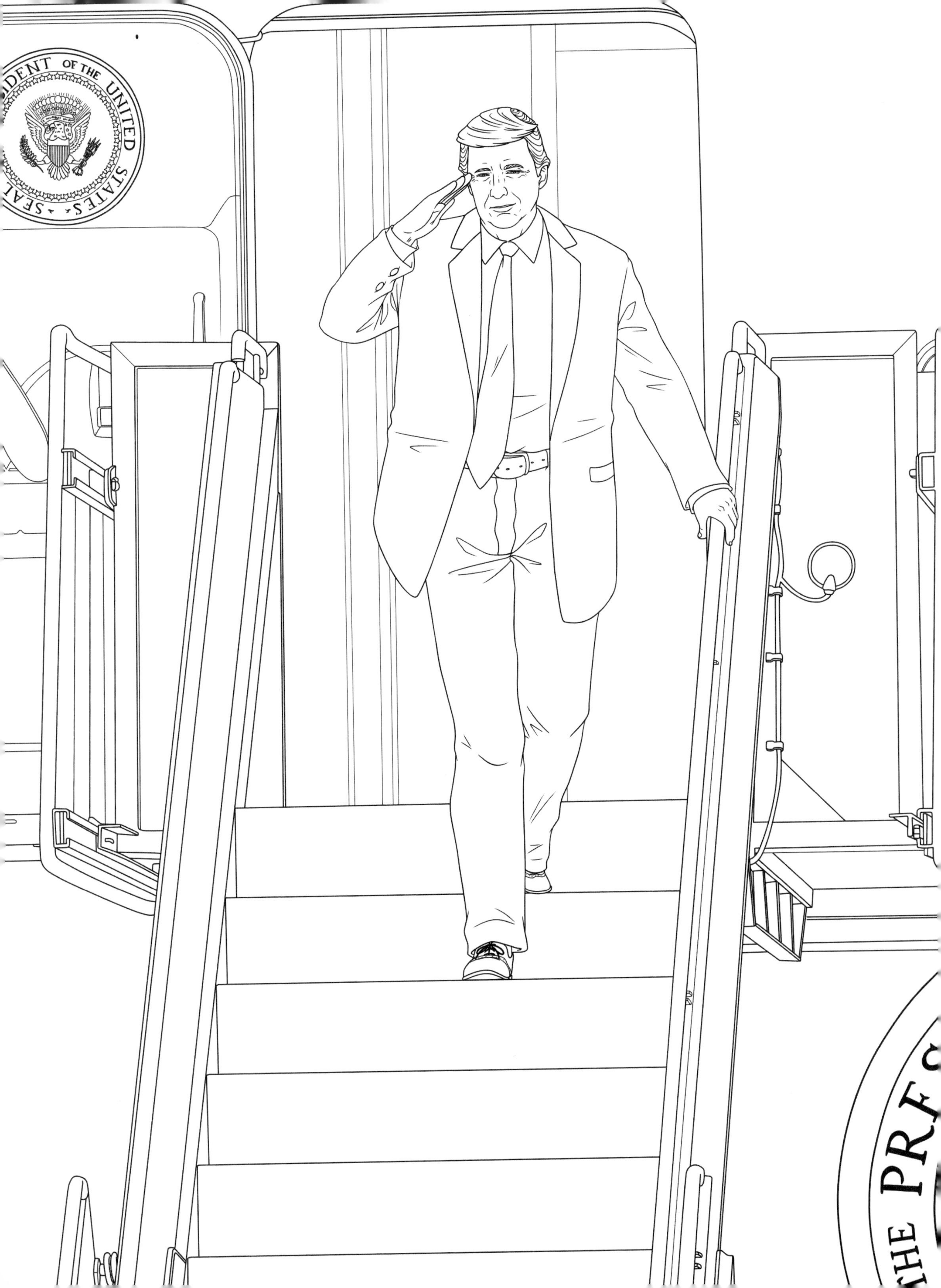
OF THE UNITED STATES
SEAL
THE

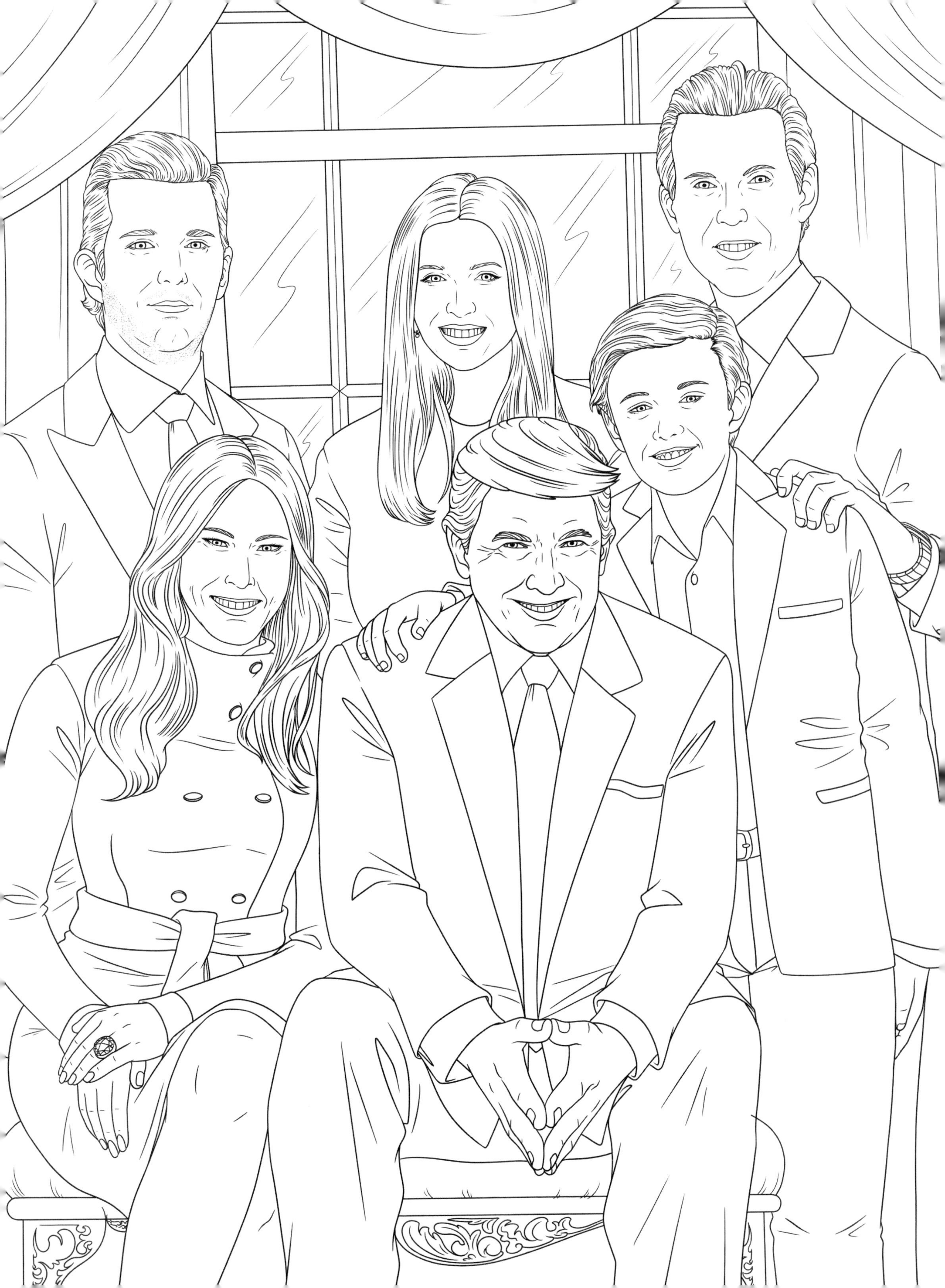

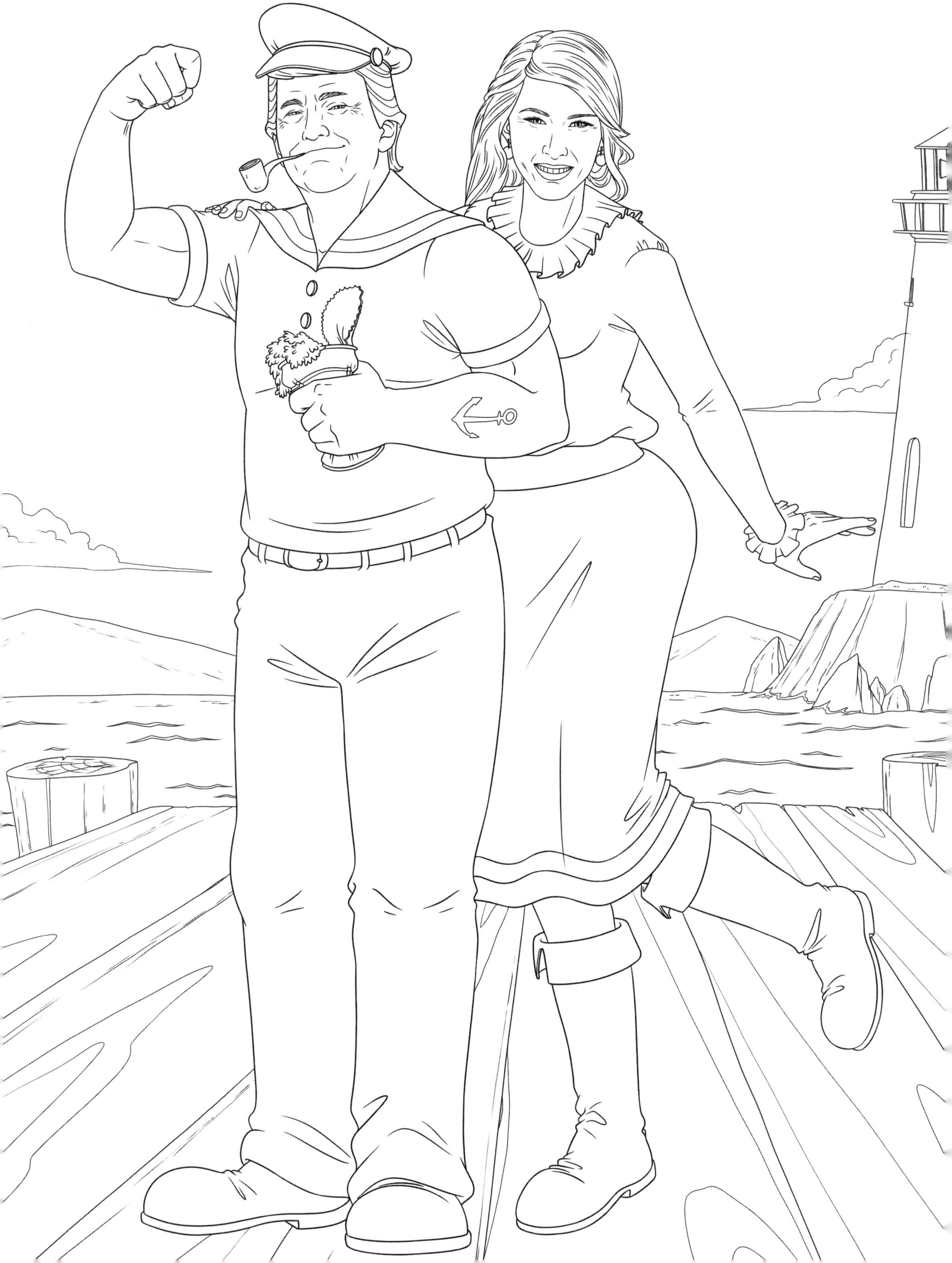

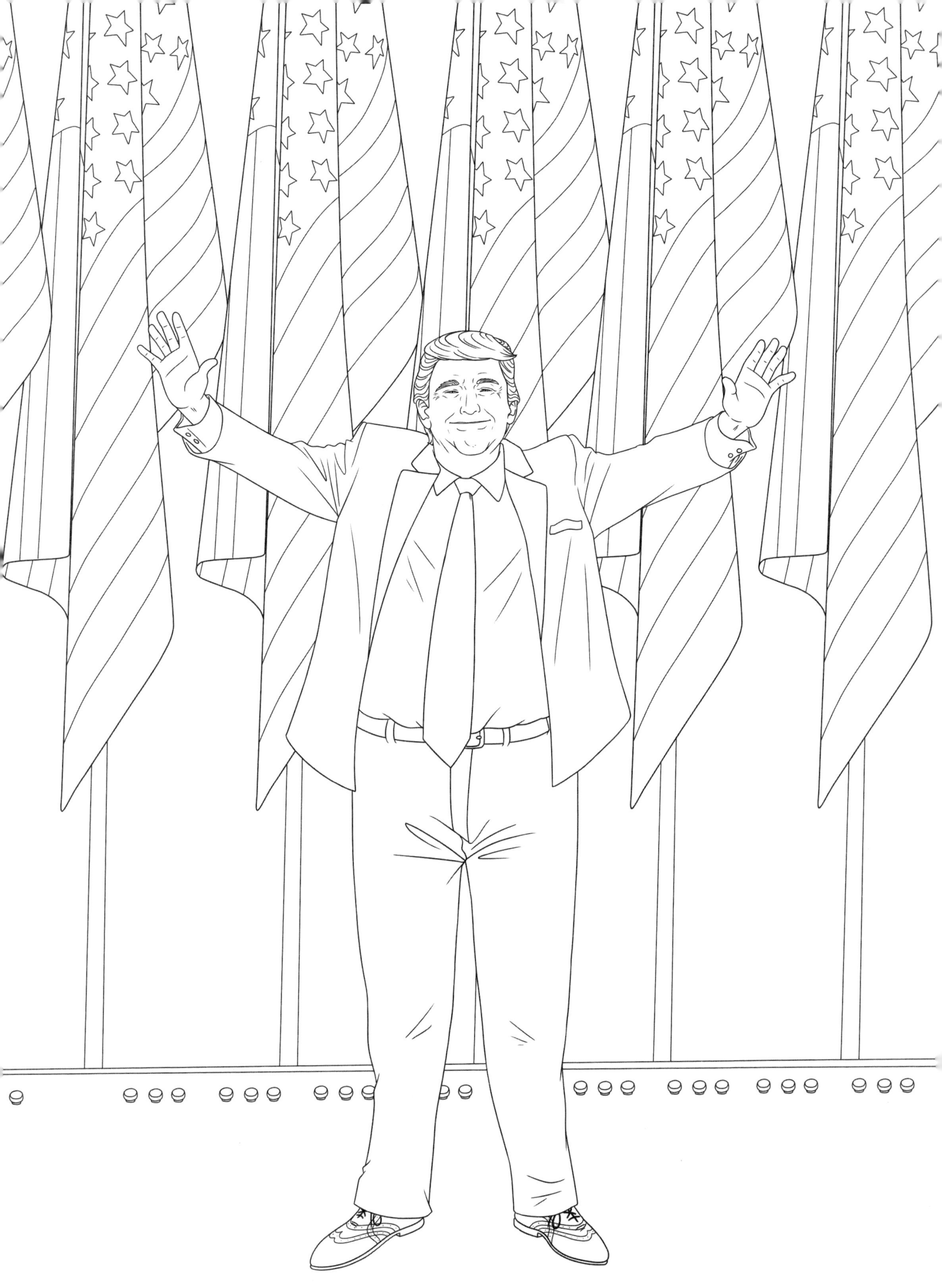

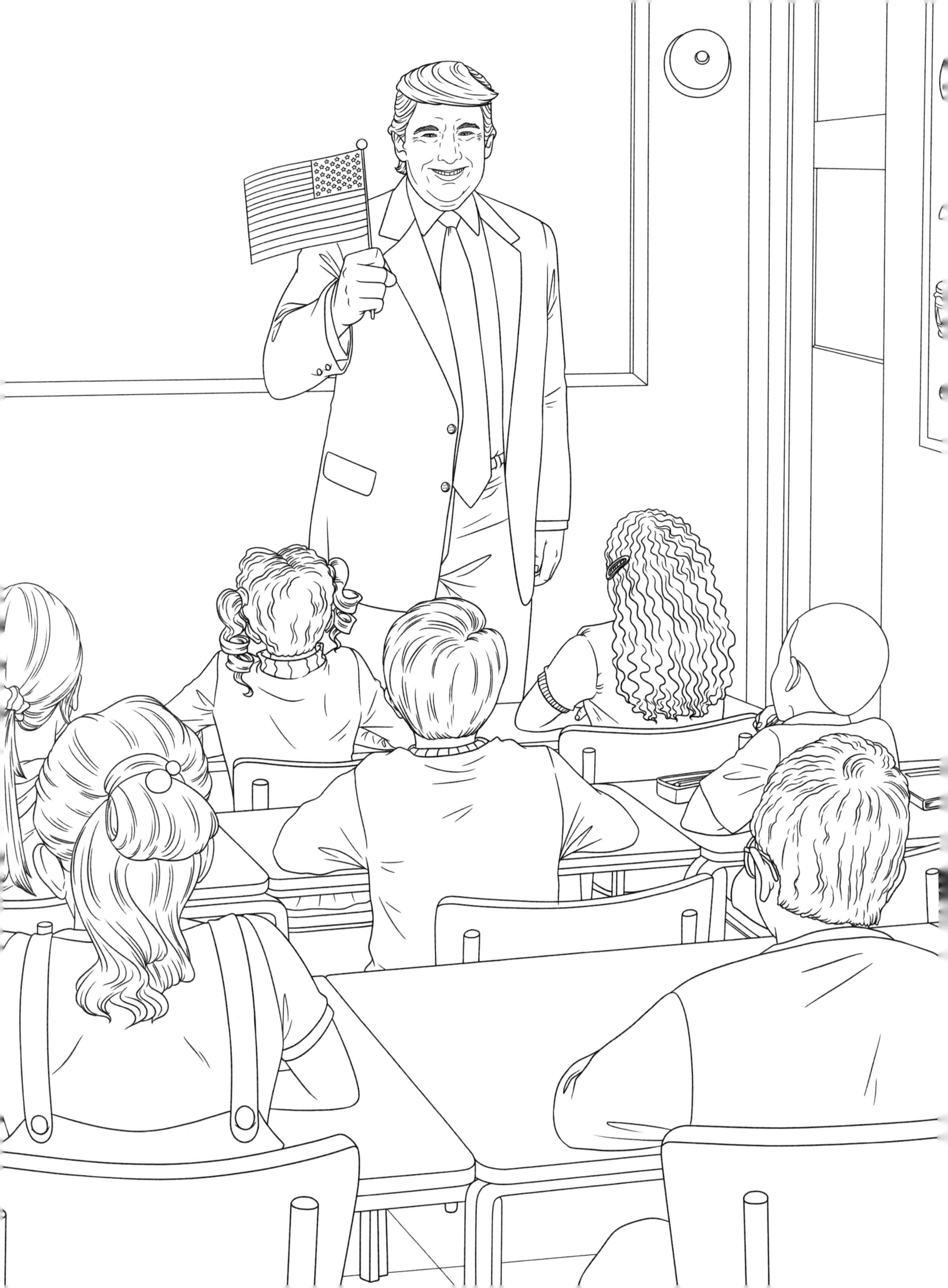

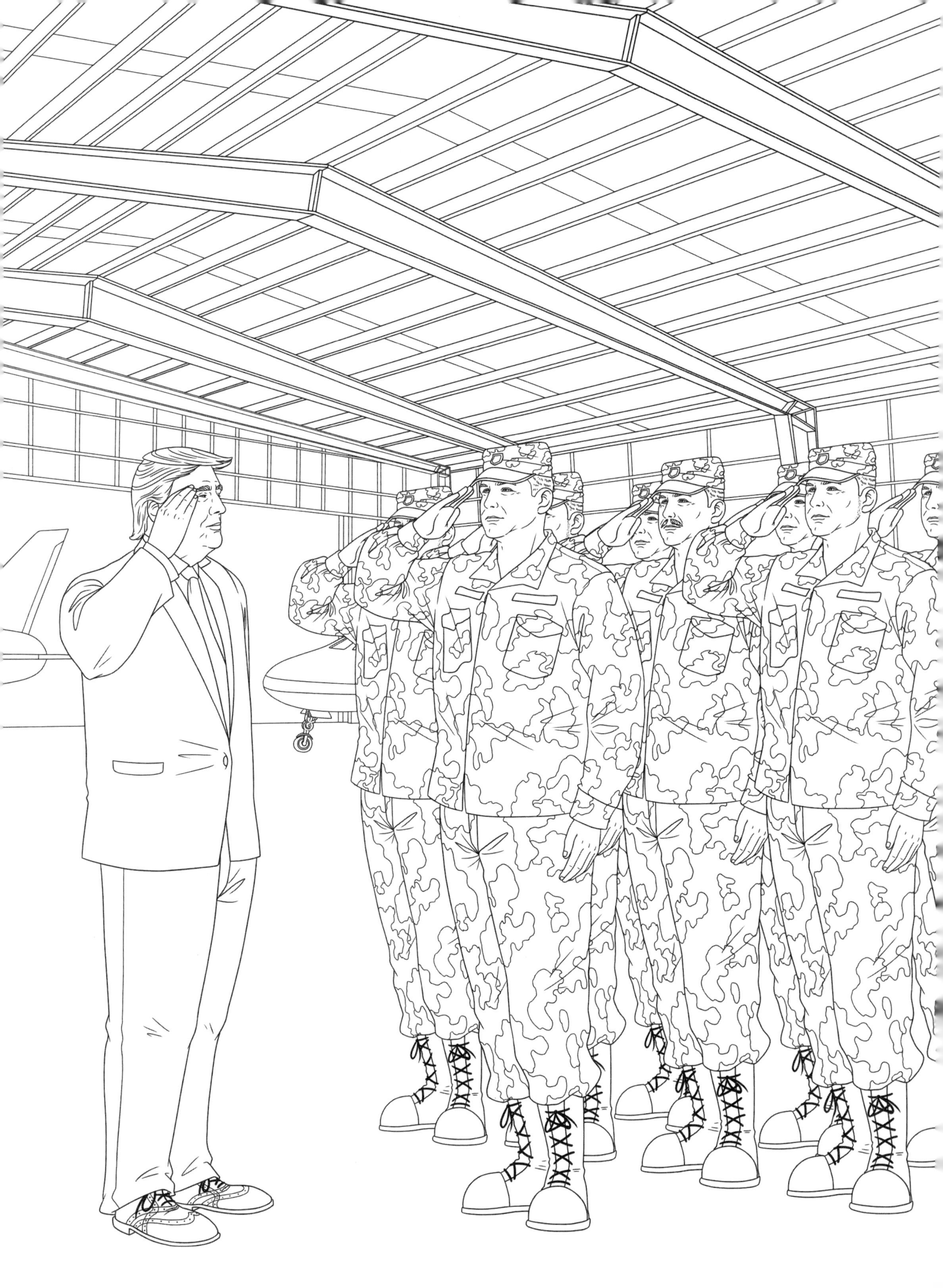

PRESIDENT
OF THE
UNITED STATES

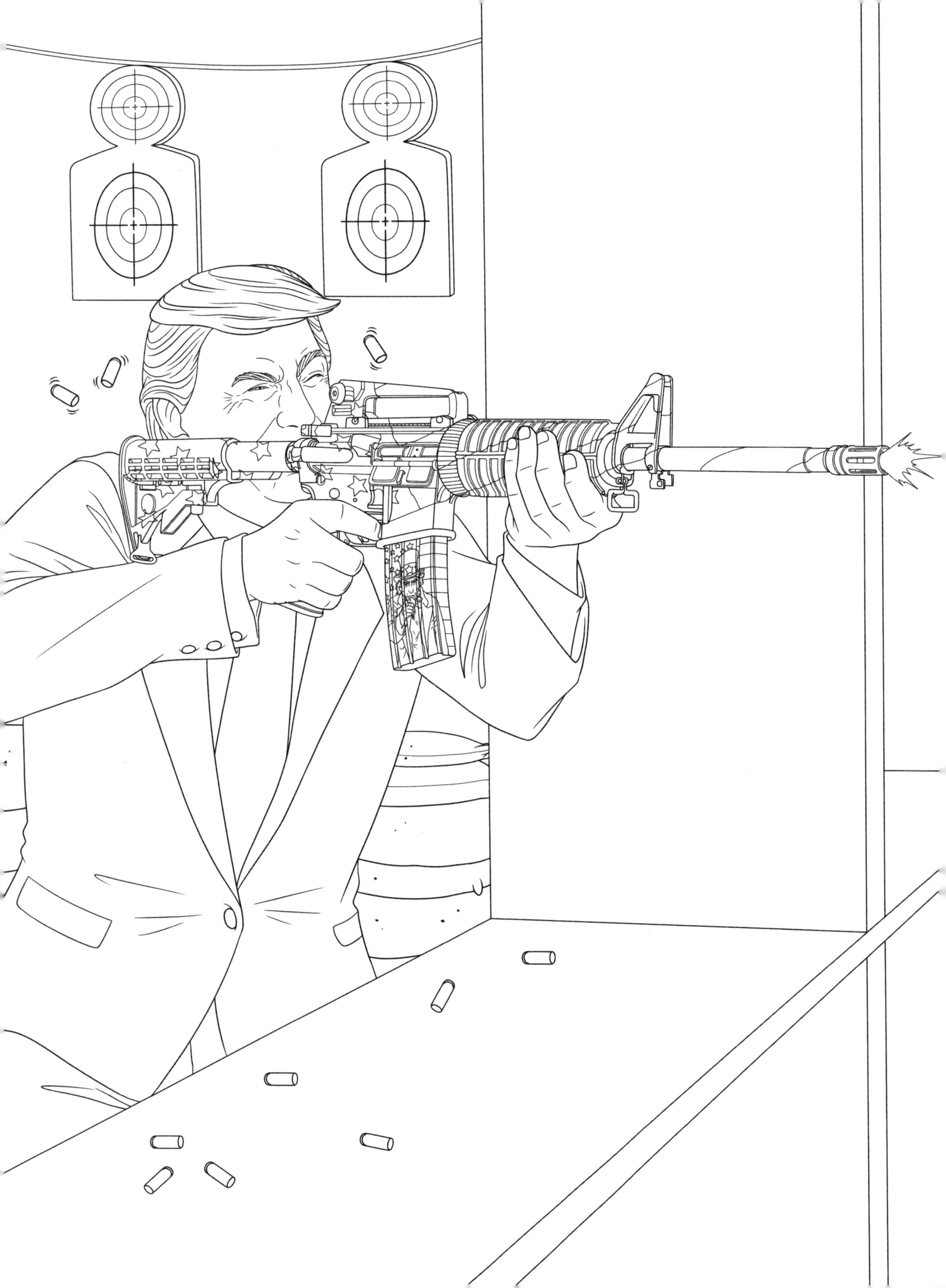

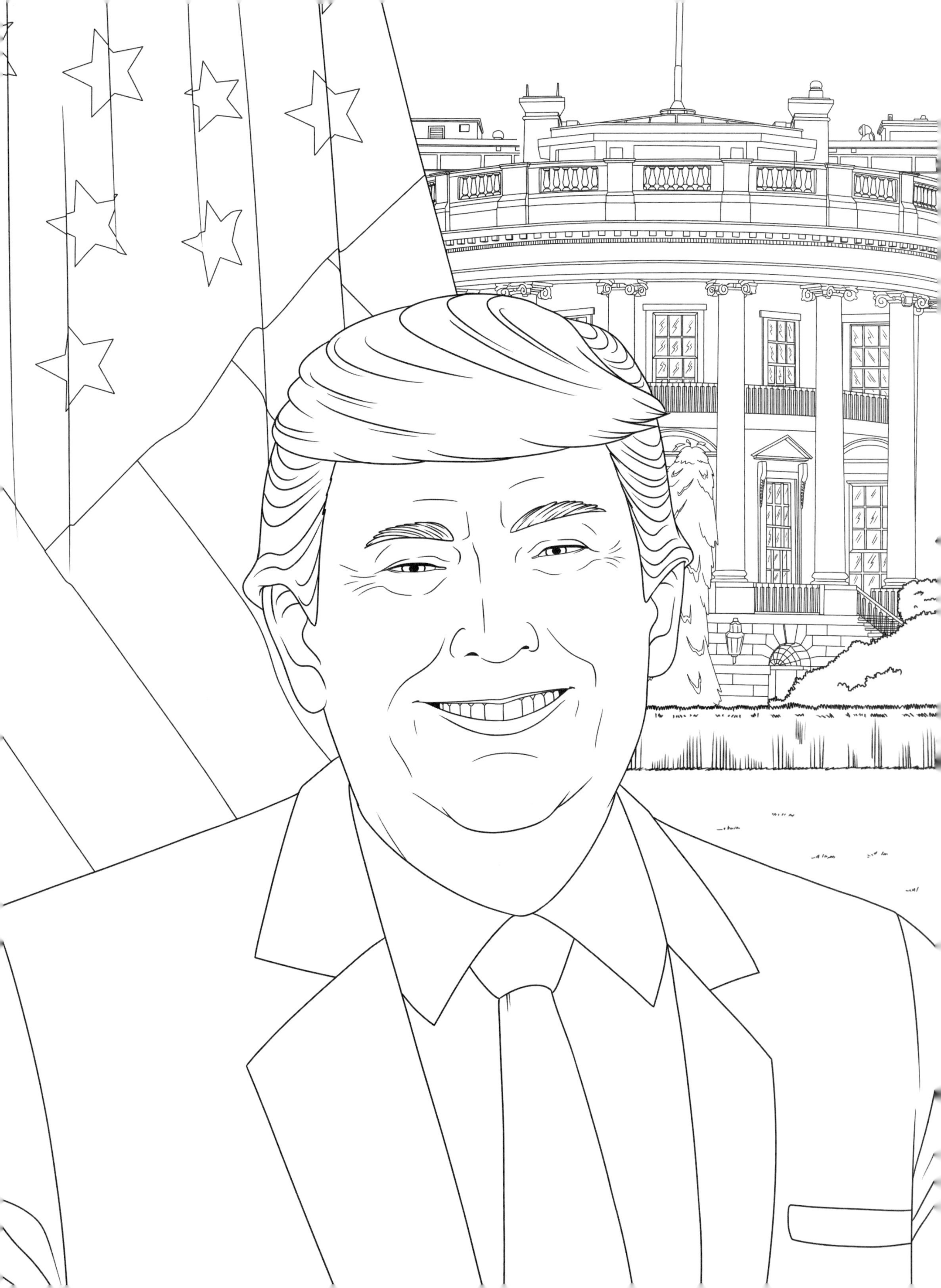

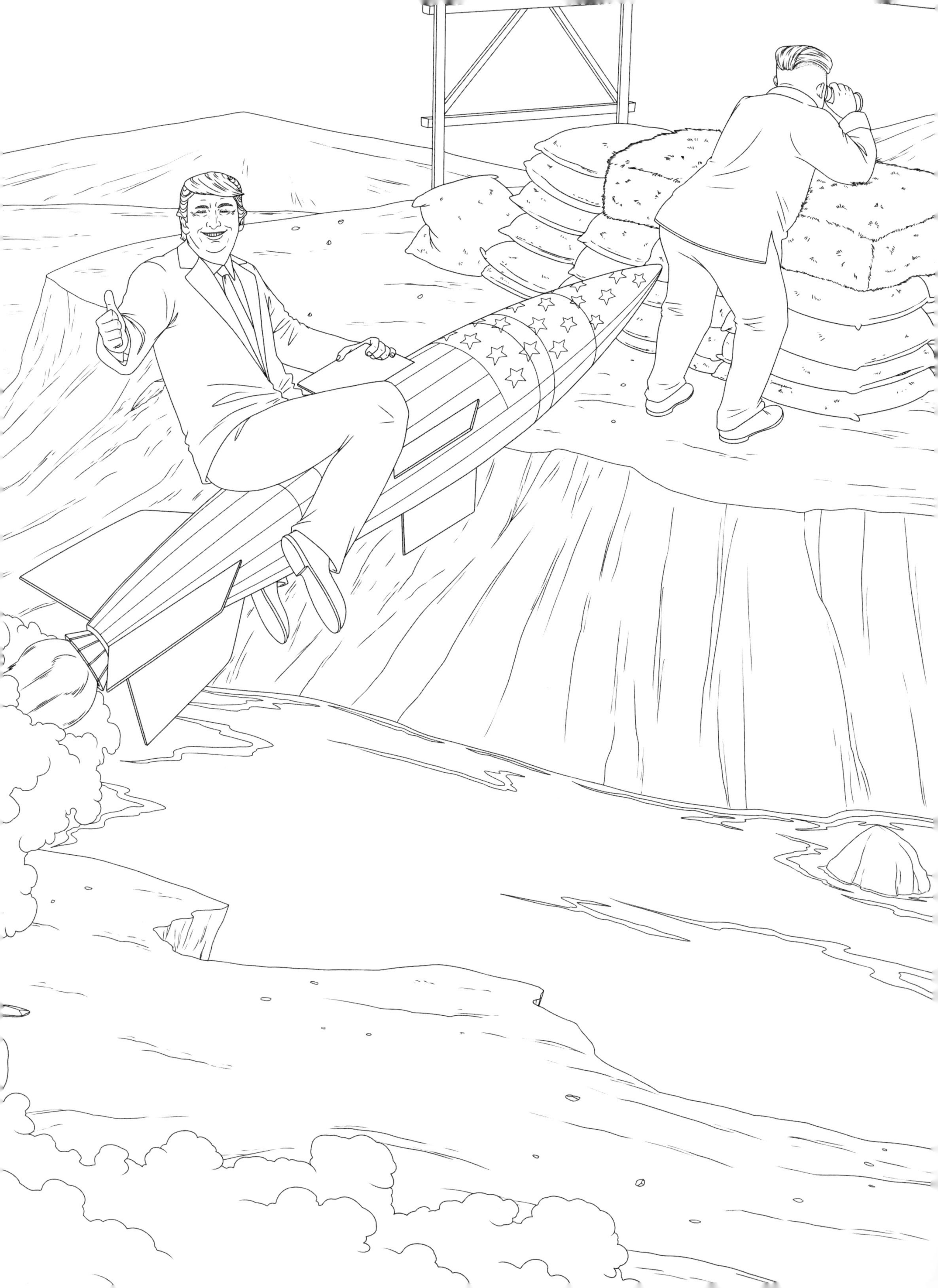

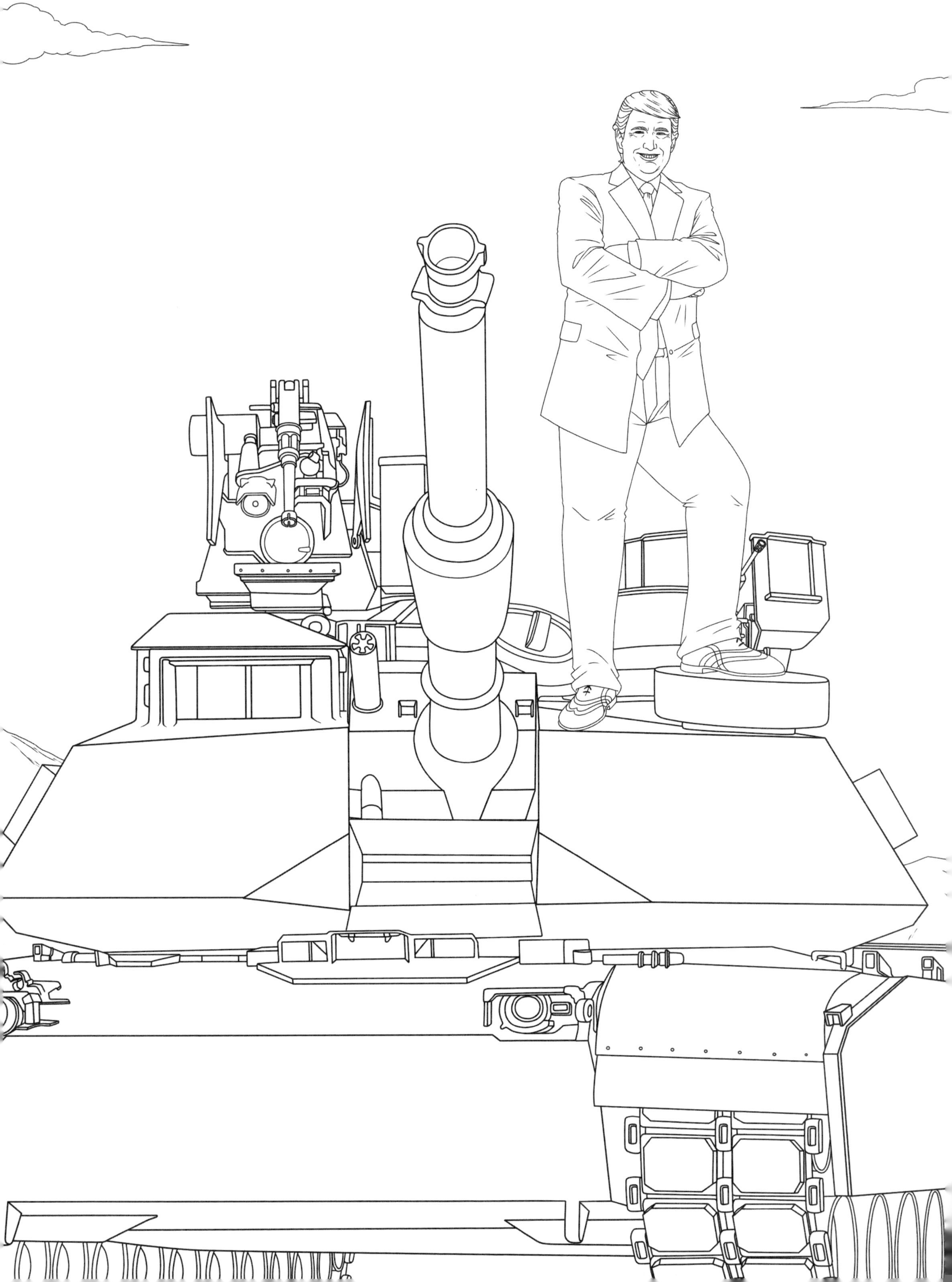

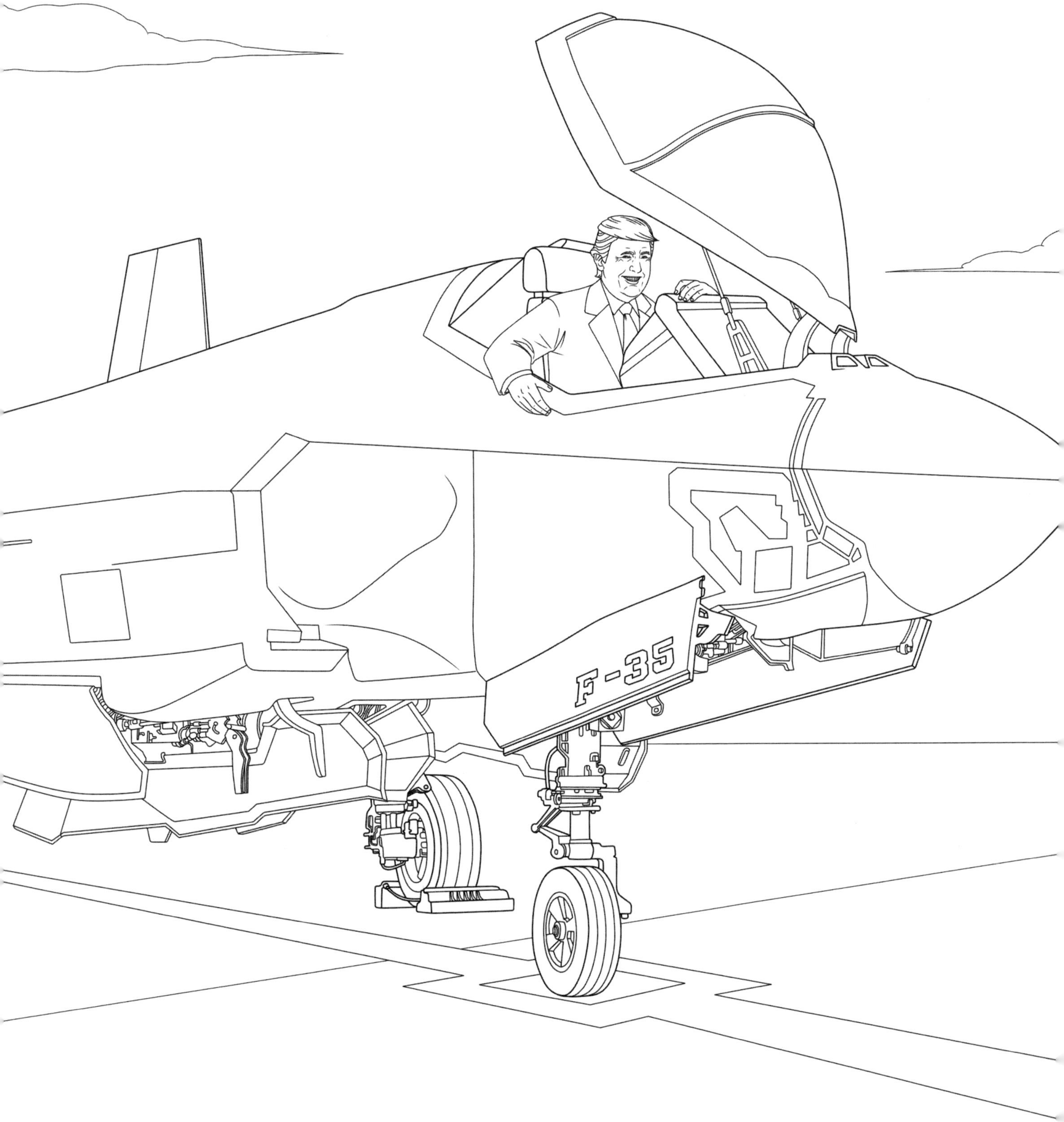
F-35

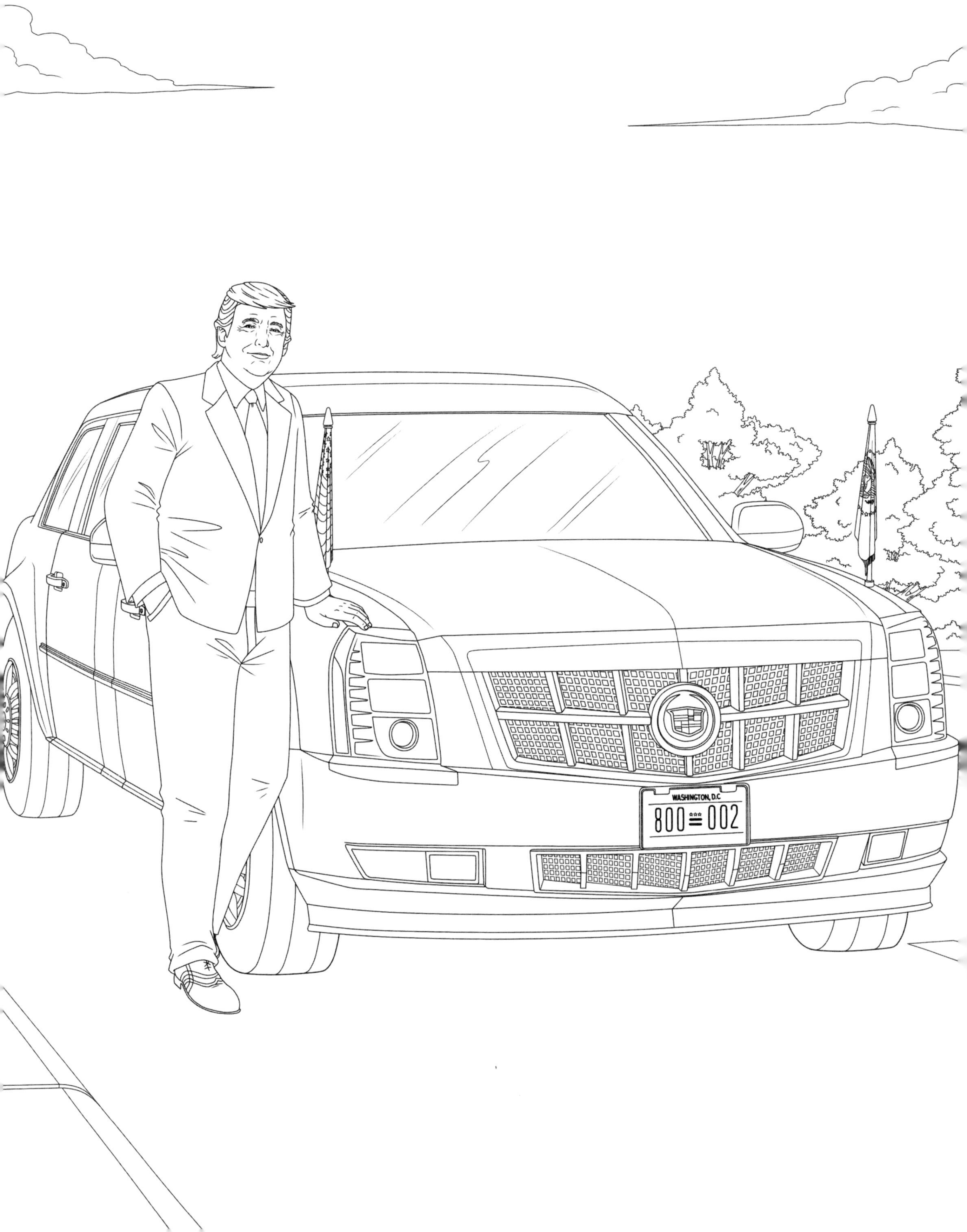
WASHINGTON, D.C
800 002

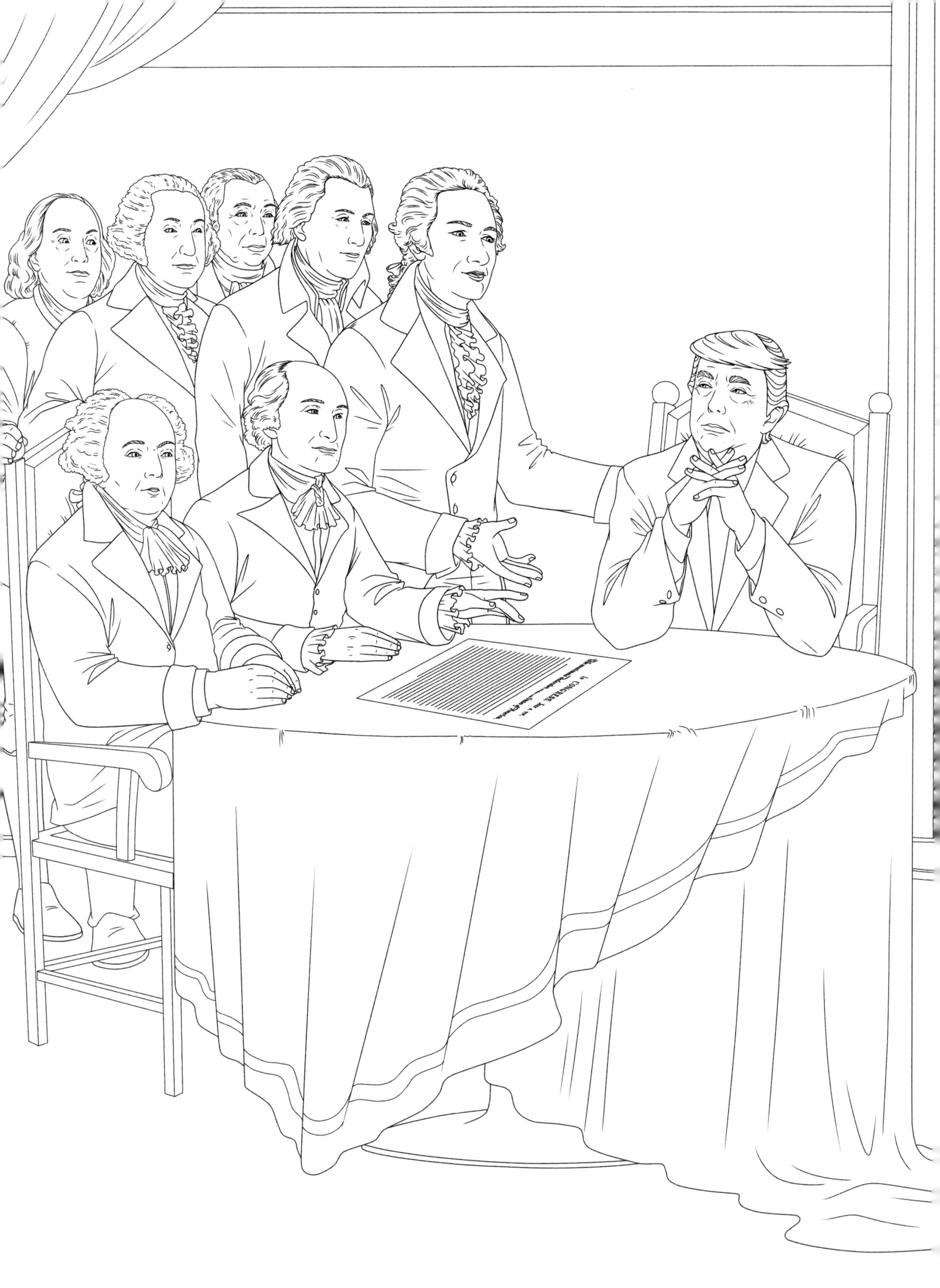
In CONGRESS,

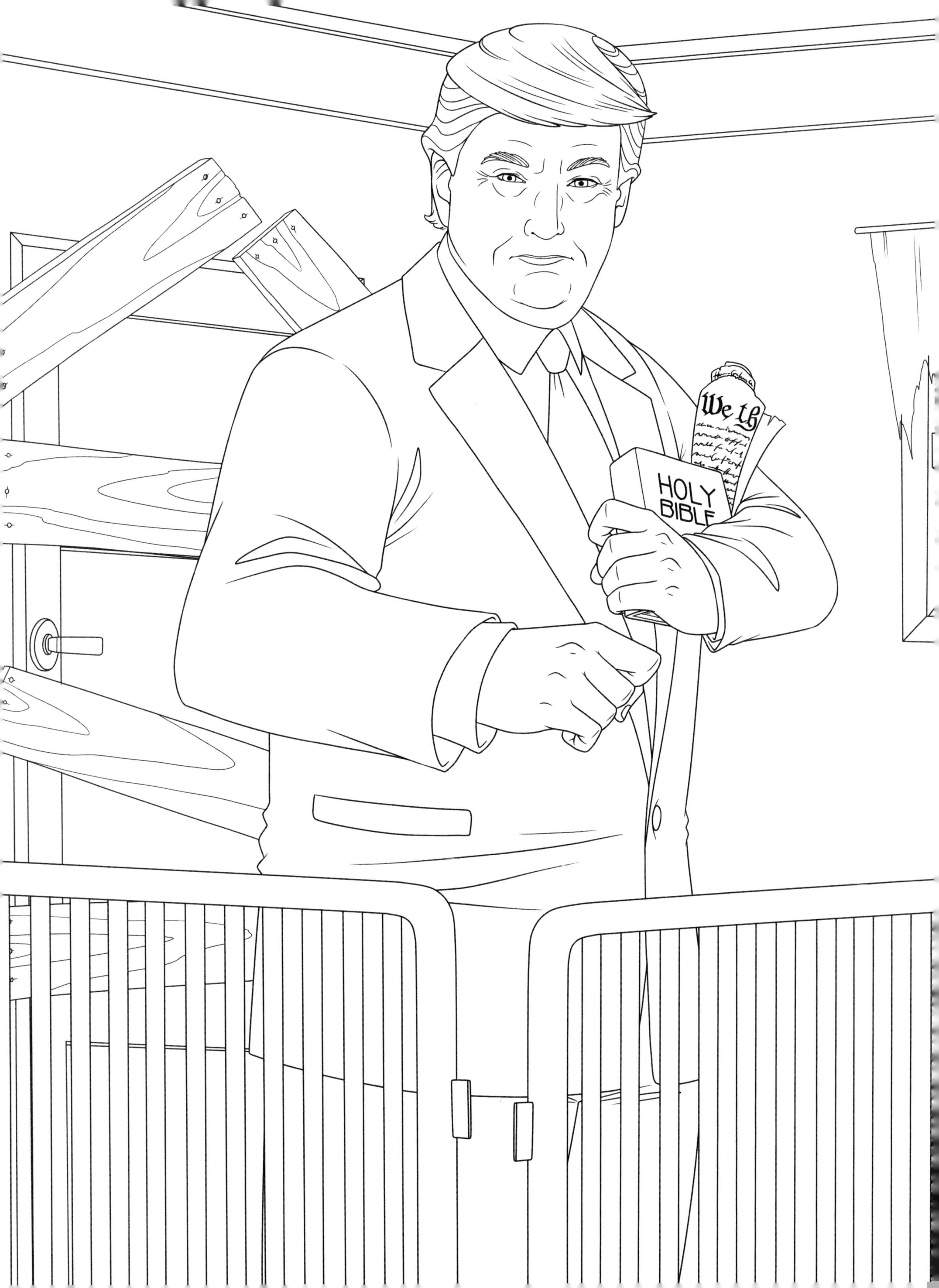
HOLY
BIBLE
We th

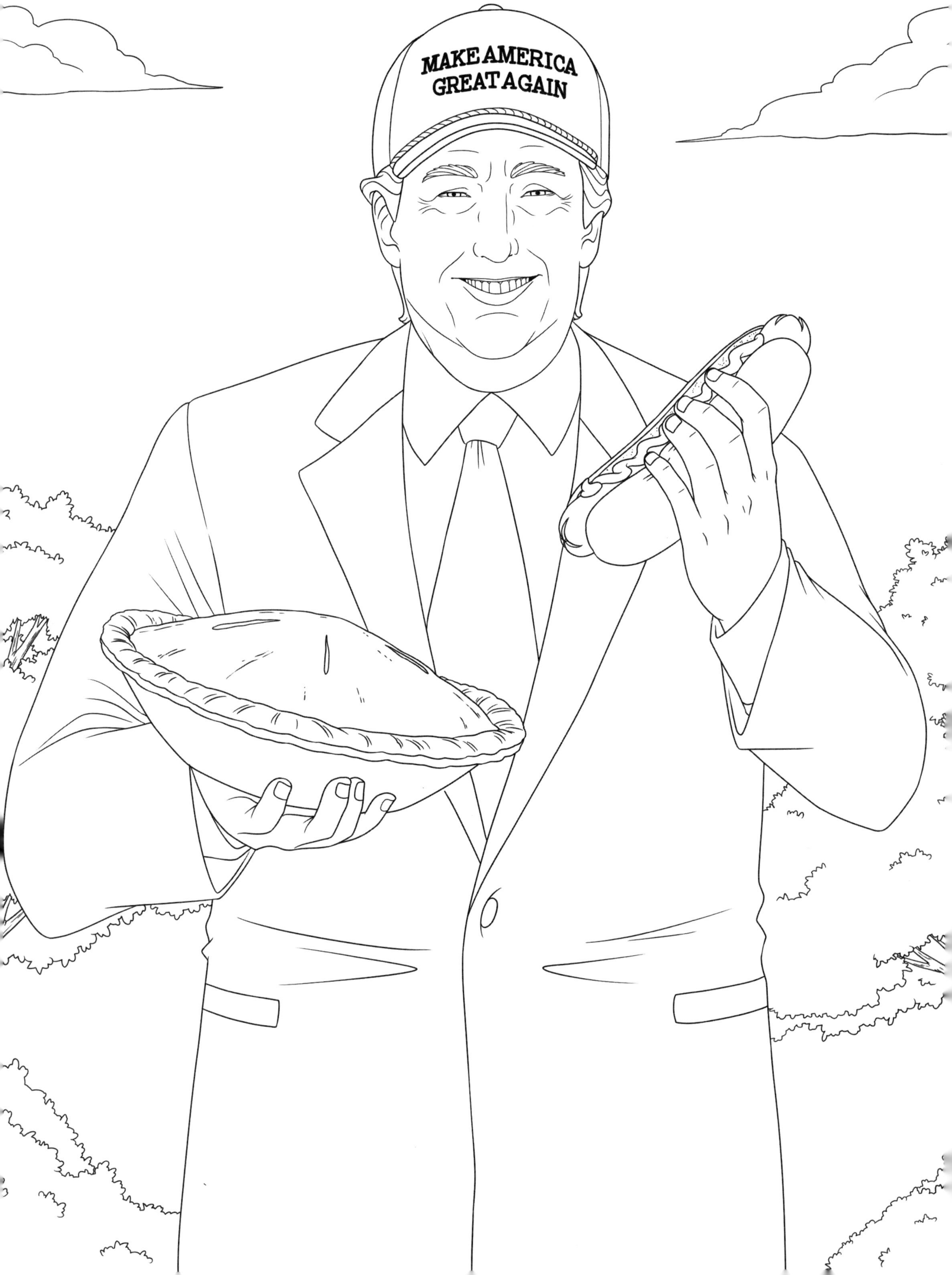
MAKE AMERICA
GREAT AGAIN

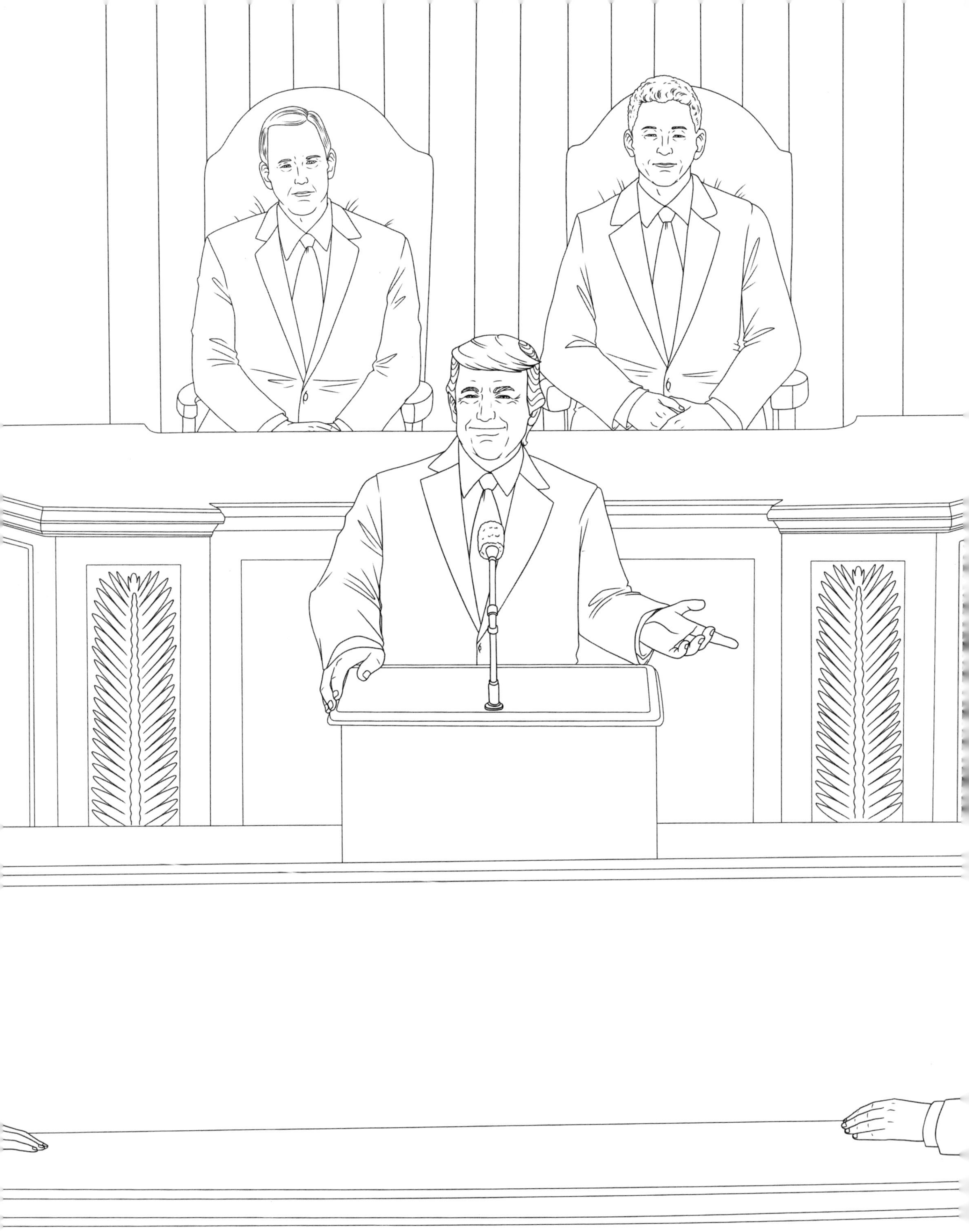

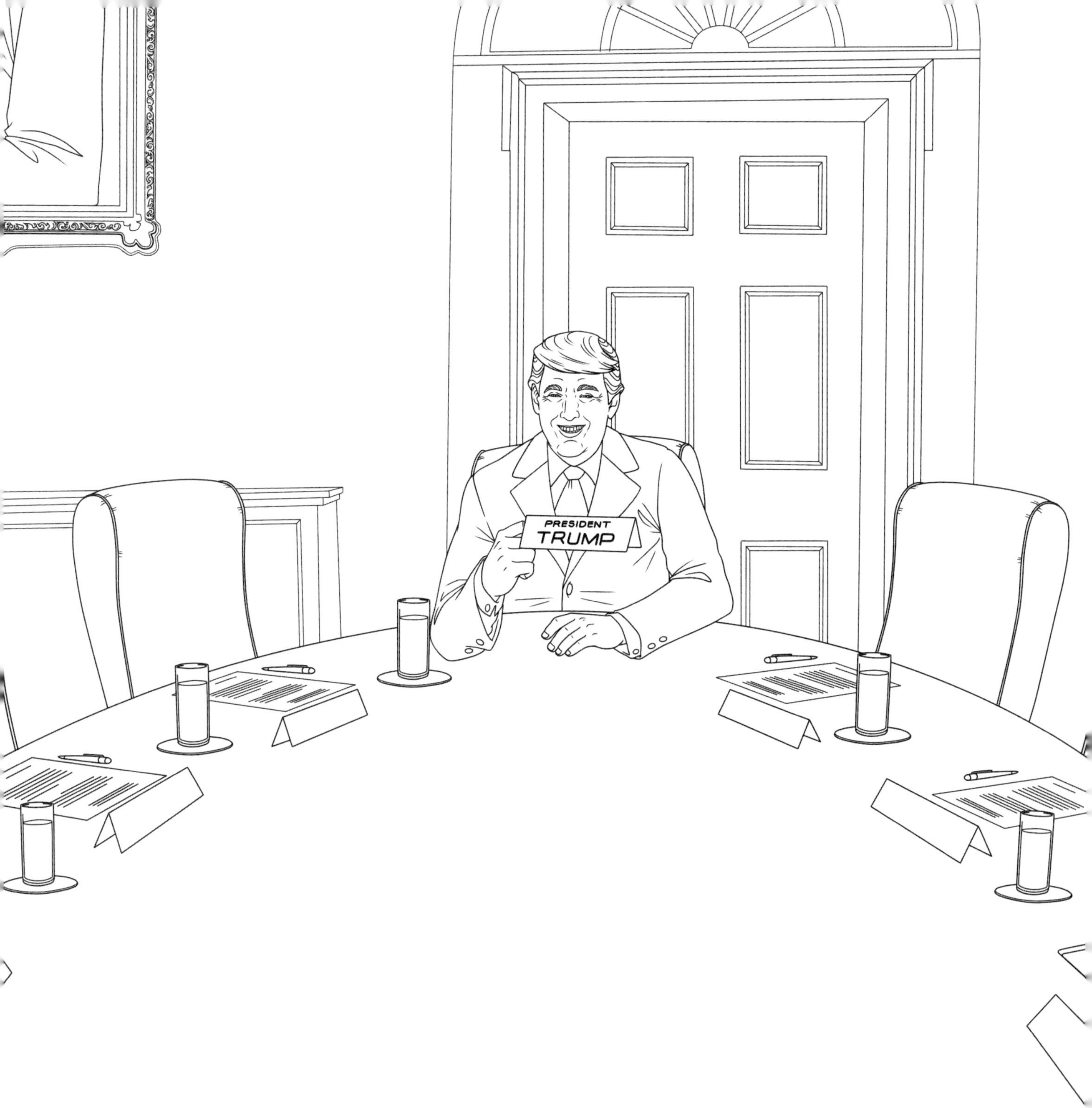
PRESIDENT
TRUMP

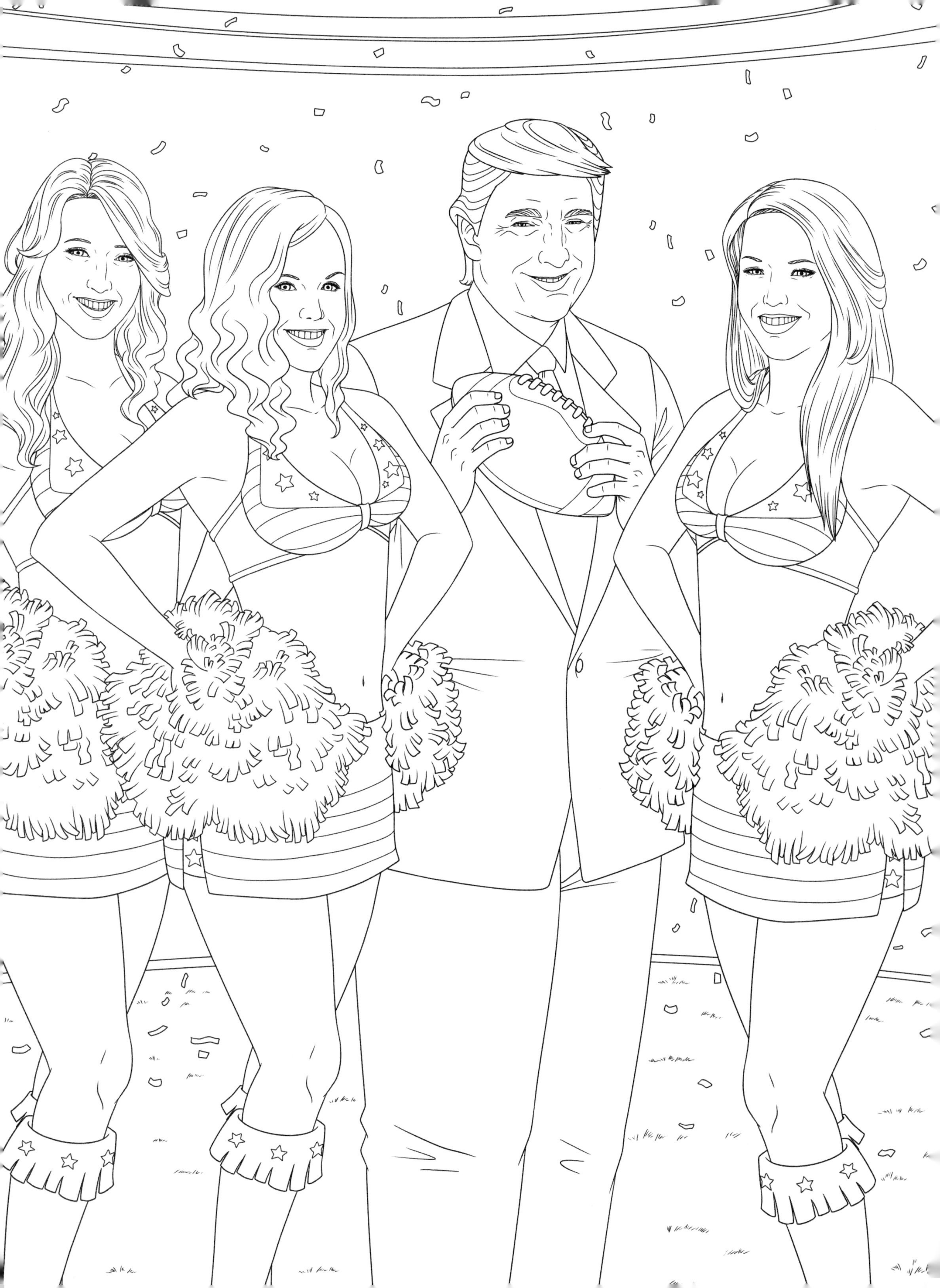

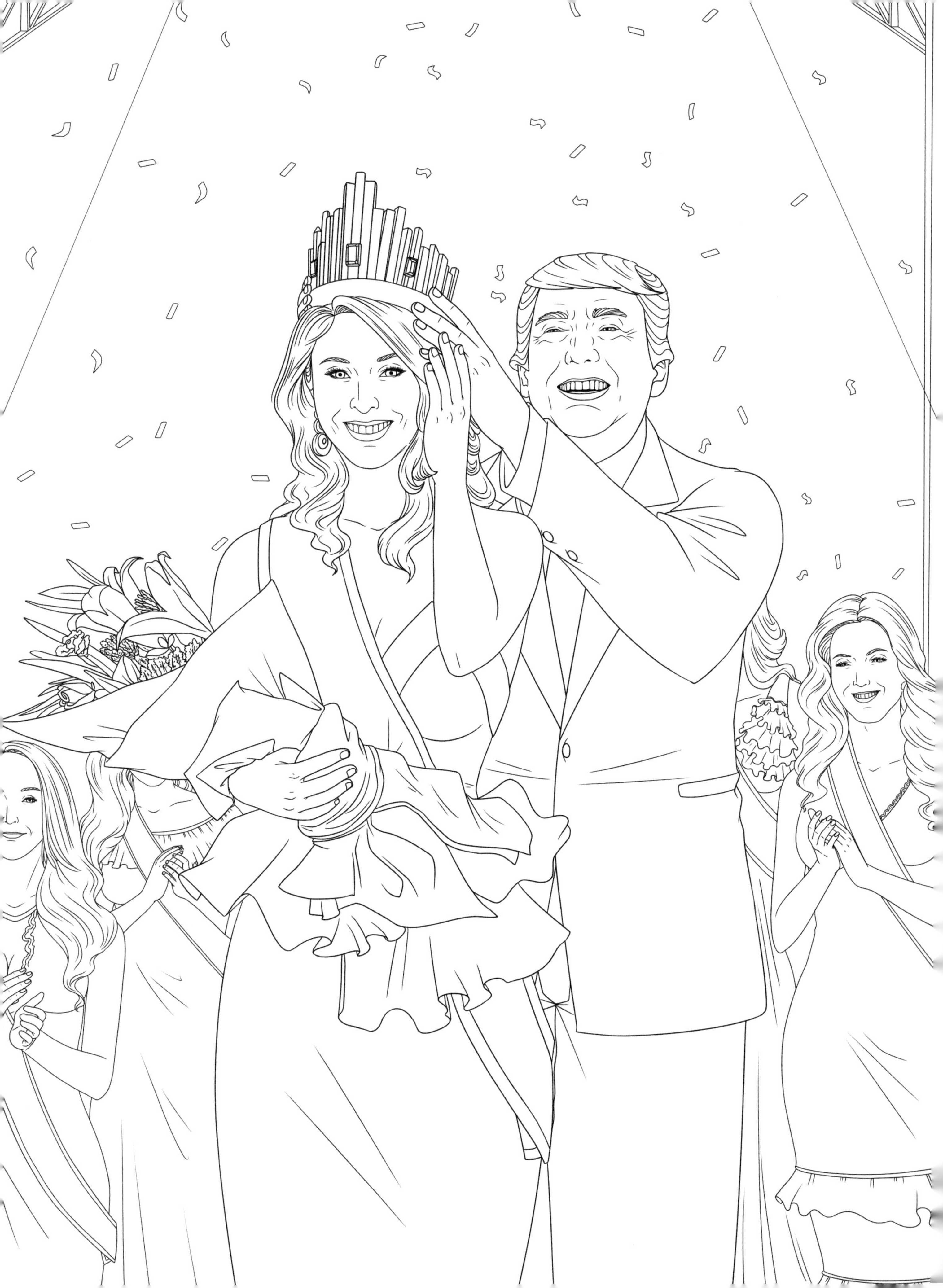

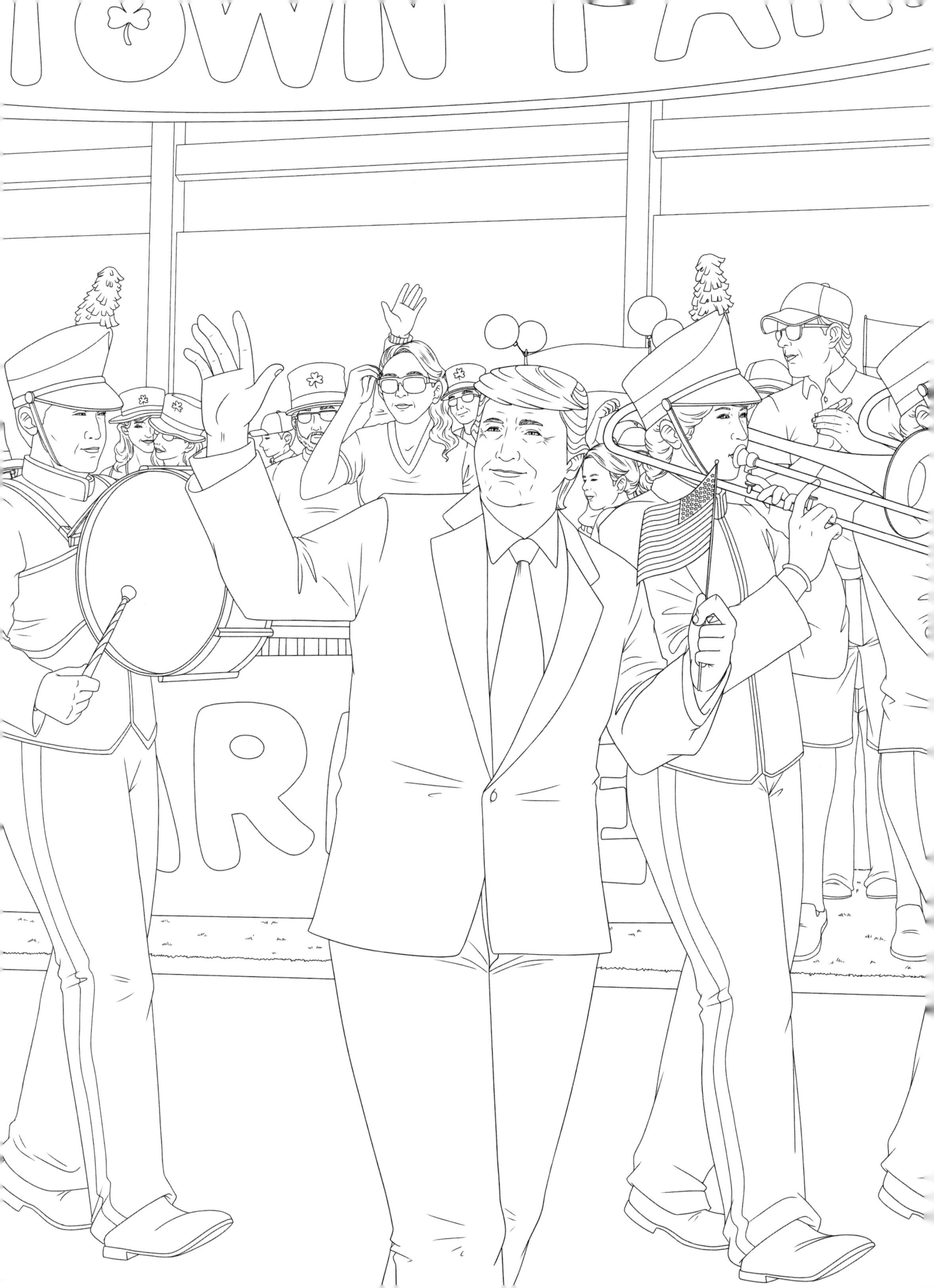